MY CREATIVE YEAR

YEAR

MARY EAKIN

HARVEST HOUSE PUBLISHERS
EUGENE, OREGON

Interior and cover design by Mary Eakin

My Creative Year
Copyright © 2019 by Mary Eakin
Published by Harvest House Publishers
Eugene, Oregon 97408
www.harvesthousepublishers.com

ISBN 978-0-7369-7564-3 (pbk.)

Mary Eakin is a graduate from the Academy of Art University of San Francisco and was an award-winning graphic designer for Hallmark's gift book division for nine years. She's also the author of *Mind Delights* and *Brain Snacks.* Mary lives with her husband and two small children in Maryland.

Printed in China

18 19 20 21 22 23 24 25 26 27 / RDS / 10 9 8 7 6 5 4 3 2 1

A YEAR'S WORTH OF INSPIRATION

Welcome.

And congratulations. You've made a great choice...

> to infuse some simple beauty into your day,
>> to refresh your soul with uplifting thoughts,
>>> and to engage your brain in some playful exercise.

Are you an accomplished artist? In these pages you'll find plenty of opportunities to sharpen your skills.

Or do you struggle simply to make recognizable stick figures? Good news—this is the perfect tool for starting right where you are and exanding your horizons.

Regardless of your artistic ability, this collection of drawing prompts, coloring pages, writing exercises, and texts to ponder is like a guided tour—a path for you to follow on your creative journey.

Where will it lead you?

> Away from tension and stress to quiet relaxation.
> Away from mindlessness and distraction to a clearer focus.
> And away from drab routines to a celebration of color and light.

It's great to have you along. Choose your own pace and enjoy the trip!

COMPLETED ACTIVITIES

(1)	2	3	4	5	6	7	8	9	10
11	12	13	14	15	16	17	18	19	20
21	22	23	24	25	26	27	28	29	30
31	32	33	34	35	36	37	38	39	40
41	42	43	44	45	46	47	48	49	50
51	52	53	54	55	56	57	58	59	60
61	62	63	64	65	66	67	68	69	70
71	72	73	74	75	76	78	79	79	80
81	82	83	84	85	86	87	88	89	90
91	92	93	94	95	96	97	98	99	100
101	102	103	104	105	106	107	108	109	110
111	112	113	114	115	116	117	118	119	120
121	122	123	124	125	126	127	128	129	130
131	132	133	134	135	136	137	138	139	140
141	142	143	144	145	146	147	148	149	150
151	152	153	154	155	156	157	158	159	160
161	162	163	164	165	166	167	168	169	170
171	172	173	174	175	176	177	178	179	180

181	182	183	184	185	186	187	188	189	190
191	192	193	194	195	196	197	198	199	200
201	202	203	204	205	206	207	208	209	210
211	212	213	214	215	216	217	218	219	220
221	222	223	224	225	226	227	228	229	230
231	232	233	234	235	236	237	238	239	240
241	242	243	244	245	246	247	248	249	250
251	252	253	254	255	256	257	258	259	260
261	262	263	264	265	266	267	268	269	270
271	272	273	274	275	276	277	278	279	280
281	282	283	284	285	286	287	288	289	290
291	292	293	294	295	296	297	298	299	300
301	302	303	304	305	306	307	308	309	310
311	312	313	314	315	316	317	318	319	320
321	322	323	324	325	326	327	328	329	330
331	332	333	334	335	336	337	338	339	340
341	342	343	344	345	346	347	348	349	350
351	352	353	354	355	356	357	358	359	360
361	362	363	364	365					

1 **DRAW** a pattern on the bird's wings.

COLOR the rainbow using several different materials, such as crayons, colored pencils, markers, and paint.

(2)

"I have set my rainbow in the clouds, and it will be the sign of the covenant between me and the earth."

GENESIS 9:13 NIV

DRAW expressive eyes on the foxes.

DRAW something from your imagination with your eyes closed.

DRAW what you wish for in the future.

"'For I know the plans I have for you,' declares the Lᴏʀᴅ, 'plans to prosper you and not to harm you, plans to give you hope and a future.'"

JEREMIAH 29:11 NIV

7 **COLOR** the raindrops with a rainbow of colors.

WRITE three places you would like to visit. **DRAW** stars around your favorite.

8

1. _____
   _____
   _____

2. _____
   _____
   _____

3. _____
   _____
   _____

"A man's heart plans his way, but the LORD directs his steps."

PROVERBS 16:9 NKJV

DRAW flowers for the bee.

"We know that God causes everything to work together for the good of those who love God and are called according to his purpose for them."

ROMANS 8:28 NLT

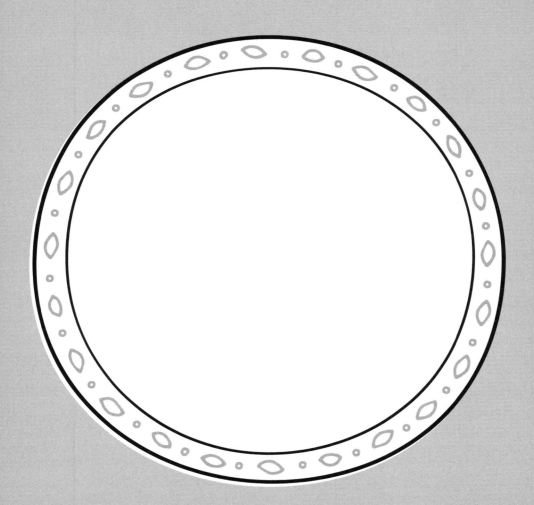

DRAW a picture in a single fluid line without picking up your pencil.

(13) In each circle, **WRITE** the name of someone who makes you laugh, and **COLOR** each circle.

"Now we see things imperfectly, like puzzling reflections in a mirror, but then we will see everything with perfect clarity. All that I know now is partial and incomplete, but then I will know everything completely, just as God now knows me completely."

1 CORINTHIANS 13:12 NLT

DRAW someone you love.

WRITE about something you accomplished this year that you're proud of. (16)

_____

_____

_____

_____

_____

_____

_____

_____

_____

_____

_____

_____

_____

_____

_____

_____

DRAW patterns in the leaves.

CONNECT the dots however you like to form an image.

DRAW something you do every morning.

"The LORD's loving kindnesses indeed never cease, for His compassions never fail. They are new every morning; great is Your faithfulness."

LAMENTATIONS 3:22-23 NASB

WRITE your favorite drinks on these mugs and **COLOR** them with your favorite colors.

20

FREE DRAW! Draw whatever you want today.

ARTIST TIP:
Use a cloth or an extra piece of paper under your
hand to avoid getting your artwork on yourself.

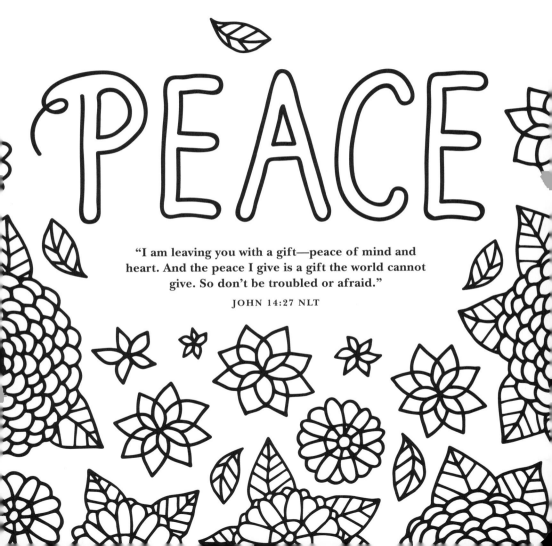

PEACE

"I am leaving you with a gift—peace of mind and heart. And the peace I give is a gift the world cannot give. So don't be troubled or afraid."

JOHN 14:27 NLT

23 **DRAW** something that bothers you. Put a large X through your drawing.

"Be strong and courageous. Do not be afraid or terrified because of them, for the LORD your God goes with you; he will never leave you nor forsake you."

DEUTERONOMY 31:6 NIV

WRITE three things you love about your life. $\left(24\right)$

1. _____
   _____
   _____

2. _____
   _____
   _____

3. _____
   _____
   _____

COLOR this autumn scene with winter colors.

DRAW your most treasured possession.

"The LORD is my shepherd; I have all that I need."

PSALM 23:1 NLT

ADD patterns to the flowers. (28)

ADD feathers to the bird and **DRAW** something it is sitting on.

COLOR this winter scene with summer colors.

30

31 **WRITE** down a line from your favorite song.
COLOR in the notes and clefs.

DRAW the first letter of your last name as large as you can fit on this page. **DECORATE** it with shapes, patterns, dots, or whatever you feel like doodling.

33 Get outside. **DRAW** something you see while taking a walk.

"Go, walk through the length and breadth of the land, for I am giving it to you."

GENESIS 13:17 NIV

COLOR the shapes using different materials.

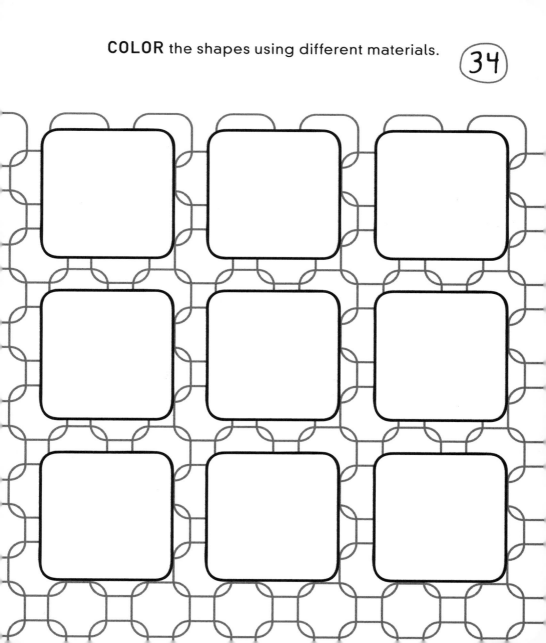

FILL this water with living creatures.

DRAW seven shells using a different color for each.

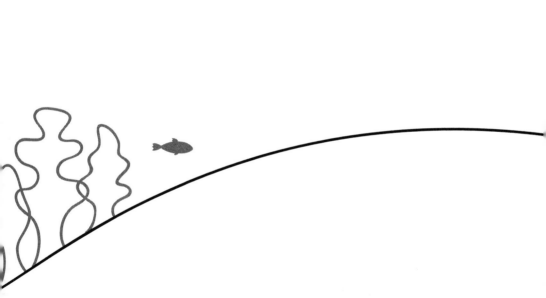

"When you pass through the waters, I will be with you;
And through the rivers, they will not overflow you."

ISAIAH 43:2 NASB

DRAW your favorite pet. If you don't have one, **DRAW** your favorite animal.

ARTIST TIP:
It's better to imperfectly doodle than to never touch the page.

FREE DRAW! Draw whatever you want today.

"Now the Lord is the Spirit, and where the Spirit of the Lord is,
there is freedom."

2 CORINTHIANS 3:17 NIV

If you are right-handed, **COLOR** the foliage with your left hand and vice versa.

"I have set the LORD continually before me;
Because He is at my right hand, I will not be shaken."

PSALM 16:8 NASB

DRAW the first thing you see after reading this.

43 COLOR the circles to make an image.

DRAW a bunch of grapes using a different color for each circle.

"Those who harvest it will eat it and praise the Lᴏʀᴅ, and those who gather the grapes will drink it in the courts of my sanctuary."

ISAIAH 62:9 NIV

45 **DRAW** something impossible.

"Jesus looked at them and said, 'With man this is impossible, but not with God; all things are possible with God.'"

MARK 10:27 NIV

FILL the sky with stars.

49 **WRITE** your favorite rainy-day activities in the raindrops. **COLOR** the picture.

DRAW what you think heaven looks like.

"In the beginning God created the heaven and the earth."

GENESIS 1:1 KJV

ADD fruit to the tree.

If you could keep only three possessions, **WRITE** what they would be.

1. _____

_____

_____

2. _____

_____

_____

3. _____

_____

_____

"Let the message of Christ dwell among you richly as you teach and admonish one another with all wisdom through psalms, hymns, and songs from the Spirit."

COLOSSIANS 3:16 NIV

53 Look outside. Is it sunny, raining, or snowing? **DRAW** the sky from what you see.

54 **DRAW** your perfect day.

COLOR the picture upside down.

DRAW patterns on the umbrellas.

"The LORD is good,
a strong refuge when trouble comes."
NAHUM 1:7 NLT

WRITE the first word that comes to your mind. Make it big! **DECORATE** the letters.

WRITE about a memorable trip you've taken.

58

DRAW faces on the flowers.

COLOR this picture moving outside the lines.

COLOR this word. **WRITE** what you like to do for fun in the loops.

WRITE about the most fun you ever had.

62

CONNECT the dots however you like to form an image.

DRAW a picture of someone you know, exaggerating their features. You could make their head extra large, their hands tiny on overly long arms. Stretch your imagination.

"You, Lord, are our Father. We are the clay, you are the potter; we are all the work of your hand."

ISAIAH 64:8 NIV

FILL in each box with a scene from each season.

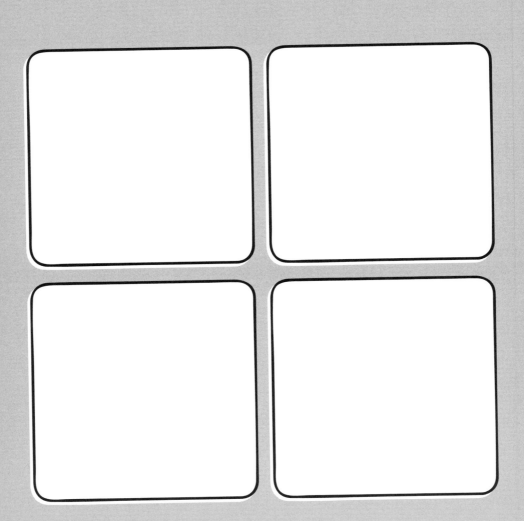

"Lᴏʀᴅ, I love the house where you live, the place where your glory dwells."

PSALM 26:8

DRAW an image using your left hand on the left side of the page and your right hand on the right side of the page.

FREE DRAW! Draw whatever you want today.

ARTIST TIP:
Want to learn how the pros do it? Many how-to art videos are available online.

WRITE three kind things others have done for you.

1 _____

_____

_____

2 _____

_____

_____

3 _____

_____

_____

"Be kind to each other, tenderhearted, forgiving one another,
just as God through Christ has forgiven you."

EPHESIANS 4:32 NLT

CREATE designs on the vases and **ADD** some flowers.

"The spirit of
man is the candle
of the LORD."

PROVERBS 20:27 KJV

DRAW a picture using only dots.

"The LORD sees clearly what a man does, examining every
path he takes."

PROVERBS 5:21 NLT

75 Complicated art usually contains some basic shapes. **CREATE** an animal or person using this circle.

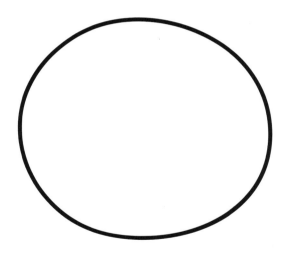

WRITE the names of people who have helped you through life on the leaves. **COLOR** them brightly.

"I thank Christ Jesus our Lord, who has given me strength to do his work."

1 TIMOTHY 1:12 NLT

DRAW a fanciful crown.

"Blessed is the one who perseveres under trial because, having stood the test, that person will receive the crown of life that the Lord has promised to those who love him."

JAMES 1:12 NIV

COLOR the picture.

78

COLOR each firefly with a different color.

CREATE a night scene on the left side of the page and the same scene in the daylight on the right.

"When Jesus spoke again to the people, he said, 'I am the light of the world. Whoever follows me will never walk in darkness, but will have the light of life.'"

JOHN 8:12 NIV

(81) **WRITE** about a time you were brave.

_____

_____

_____

_____

_____

_____

_____

_____

_____

_____

_____

_____

_____

_____

_____

"Watch, stand fast in the faith, be brave, be strong.
Let all that you do be done with love."

1 CORINTHIANS 16:13-14 NKJV

"The LORD is gracious, and full of compassion; slow to anger, and of great mercy."

PSALM 145:8 KJV

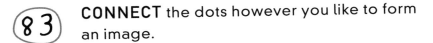

CONNECT the dots however you like to form an image.

(83)

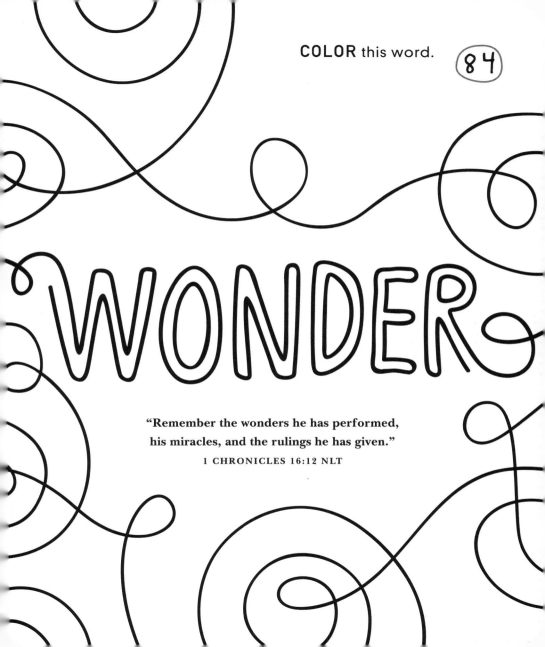

"Remember the wonders he has performed,
his miracles, and the rulings he has given."

1 CHRONICLES 16:12 NLT

(8 5)   **DRAW** a joyous forest.

"Let the trees of the forest sing for joy before the LORD."

1 CHRONICLES 16:33 NLT

FILL this page with hearts with no two alike.

"Glory in His holy name;
Let the hearts of those rejoice who seek the Lord!"

1 CHRONICLES 16:10 NKJV

DRAW different eyewear on the deer.

"His glory covered the heavens and his praise filled the earth.
His splendor was like the sunrise; rays flashed from his hand,
where his power was hidden."

HABAKKUK 3:3-4 NIV

ADD leaves to the tree.

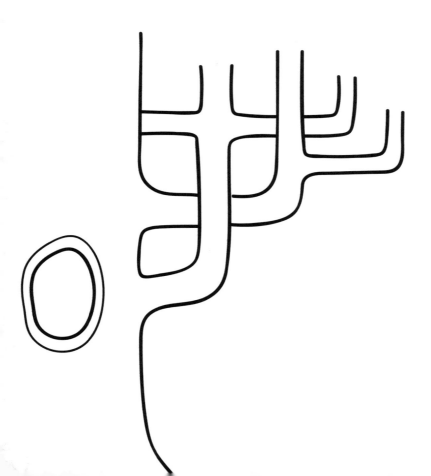

_____

_____

_____

_____

_____

_____

_____

_____

_____

_____

_____

_____

_____

_____

COLOR the triangles to make an image.

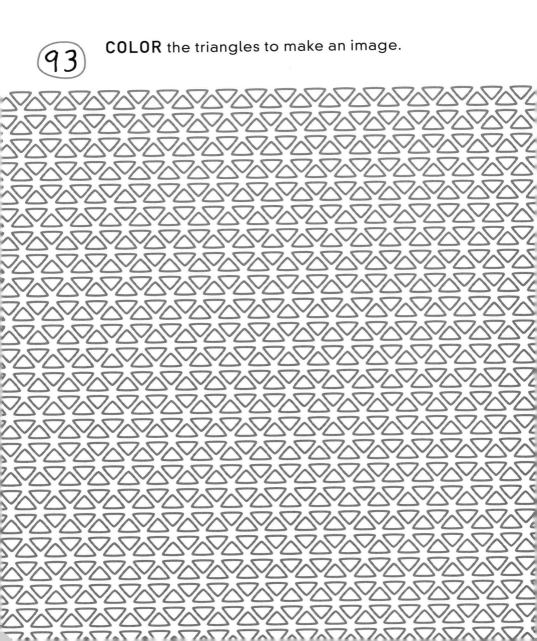

DRAW something you find beautiful in another country. It could be art, fashion, architecture, people, or a landscape.

"Many nations shall be joined to the LORD in that day, and they shall become My people. And I will dwell in your midst. Then you will know that the LORD of hosts has sent Me to you."

ZECHARIAH 2:11 NKJV

95 Start a conversation with someone and **DOODLE** here while you talk.

ARTIST TIP:
Bring a sketch book with you when you
go out. Inspiration can strike anywhere.

(97) **WRITE** about a place you would like to visit in history.

_____
_____
_____
_____
_____
_____
_____
_____
_____
_____
_____
_____
_____
_____

PRACTICE drawing hands—open, closed, and making different gestures.

"The heavens are telling of the glory of God;
And their expanse is declaring the work of His hands."

PSALM 19:1 NASB

99 FREE DRAW! Create whatever you want today.

....

100 COLOR the picture.

DRAW seven clouds with no two alike.

. . . .

DRAW an unbreakable shield.

"It is You who blesses the righteous man, O LORD,
You surround him with favor as with a shield."

PSALM 5:12 NASB

103 Anything can be given character. **DRAW** a large teapot; **ADD** spots, stripes, eyeballs, fur, wings, or whatever you can imagine.

ARTIST TIP:
Show your artwork to a friend to get a new perspective you may not have thought of.

CONNECT the dots however you like to form an image.

105 **WRITE** about a time you helped someone in need.

_____

_____

_____

_____

_____

_____

_____

_____

_____

_____

_____

_____

_____

_____

_____

_____

DRAW your favorite foods from nature.

"Look at the birds. They don't plant or harvest or store food in barns, for your heavenly Father feeds them. And aren't you far more valuable to him than they are?"

MATTHEW 6:26 NLT

FINISH this drawing.

Complicated art usually contains some basic shapes. **CREATE** an animal or person using this square.

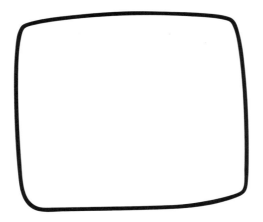

DRAW ten flowers with no two alike.

DRAW something you find restful.

"You have six days each week for your ordinary work,
but on the seventh day you must stop working, even during the
seasons of plowing and harvest."

EXODUS 34:21 NLT

With paint or a washable stamp pad, **CREATE** art on this page using only your fingertips.

115 Anything can be given character. **DRAW** a car. Make it big! **ADD** spots, stripes, eyeballs, fur, wings, or whatever your imagination comes up with.

"Whatever you do, do your work heartily, as for the Lord rather than for men."

COLOSSIANS 3:23 NASB

COLOR the bird using several different materials.

FINISH the sentence: This year I will...

① _____
_____
_____
_____

② _____
_____
_____
_____

③ _____
_____
_____
_____

ADD fruit to the basket.

"You will eat the fruit of your labor; blessings and prosperity will be yours."

PSALM 128:2 NIV

COLOR the bees in six different color combinations.

TRACE your hand. **DRAW** an important scene from your life inside.

ARTIST TIP:
Listening to your favorite music while you draw can help put you into a creative mood.

COLOR this word.

121

"Jesus left there and went along the Sea of Galilee. Then he went up on a mountainside and sat down. Great crowds came to him, bringing the lame, the blind, the crippled, the mute and many others, and laid them at his feet; and he healed them."

MATTHEW 15:29-30 NIV

CONNECT the dots however you like to form an image.

WRITE about someone who gives you encouragement. 124

"Encourage one another and build each other up, just as in fact you are doing."

1 THESSALONIANS 5:11 NIV

FINISH this drawing.

ADD a pattern to the blanket.

COLOR around the Scripture.

"They that wait upon the LORD shall renew their strength; they shall mount up with wings as eagles; they shall run, and not be weary; and they shall walk, and not faint."

ISAIAH 40:31 KJV

FILL the page with leaves, no two alike.

"Trust in your money and down you go! But the godly flourish like
leaves in spring."

PROVERBS 11:28 NLT

PRACTICE drawing eyes and eyebrows with different expressions.

FILL this heart with things you are thankful for. (130)

"Let the peace of Christ rule in your hearts, to which indeed you
were called in one body; and be thankful."

COLOSSIANS 3:15 NASB

COLOR the picture.

WRITE about what gives you peace.

$$\overline{\hspace{9cm}}$$

"Make every effort to live in peace with everyone and to be holy;
without holiness no one will see the Lord."

HEBREWS 12:14 NIV

133 **DRAW** yourself drawing yourself.

LIST your favorite things starting with each letter of the alphabet.

A _____   N _____

B _____   O _____

C _____   P _____

D _____   Q _____

E _____   R _____

F _____   S _____

G _____   T _____

H _____   U _____

I _____   V _____

J _____   W _____

K _____   X _____

L _____   Y _____

M _____   Z _____

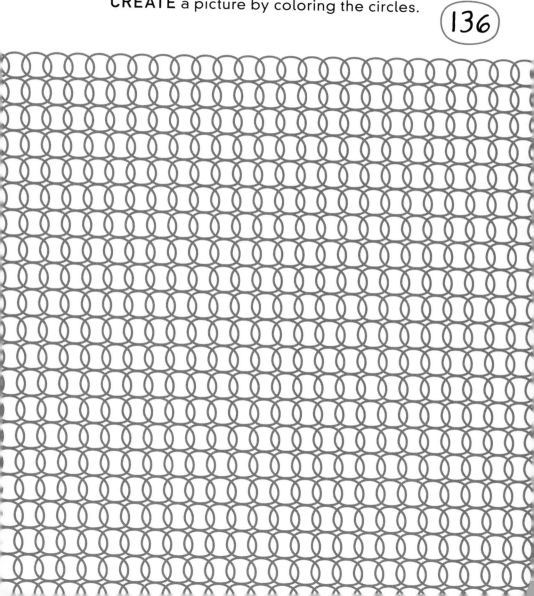

(137) **WRITE** what you would say to your younger self.

Anything can be given character. **DRAW** a shoe large and **ADD** spots, stripes, eyeballs, fur, wings, or whatever your imagination comes up with.

FREE DRAW! Draw whatever you want today.

FREE WRITE! Write whatever you want today.

COLOR this word.

"The Holy Spirit produces this kind of fruit in our lives: love, joy, peace, patience, kindness, goodness, faithfulness, gentleness, and self-control."

GALATIANS 5:22-23 NLT

DRAW something good for all people.

"See that no one repays another with evil for evil, but always seek after that which is good for one another and for all people."

1 THESSALONIANS 5:15 NASB

CONNECT the dots however you like to form an image.

DRAW a picture upside down.

ARTIST TIP:
A good night's sleep, good food, candles...
nurture your creative spirit.

CREATE something using this Scripture as inspiration.

"Wherever your treasure is, there the desires of your heart will also be."

LUKE 12:34 NLT

146

COLOR around the Scripture.

"Have I not told you? Be strong and have strength of heart! Do not be afraid or lose faith. For the Lord your God is with you anywhere you go."

JOSHUA 1:9 NLV

DRAW faces on the squares.

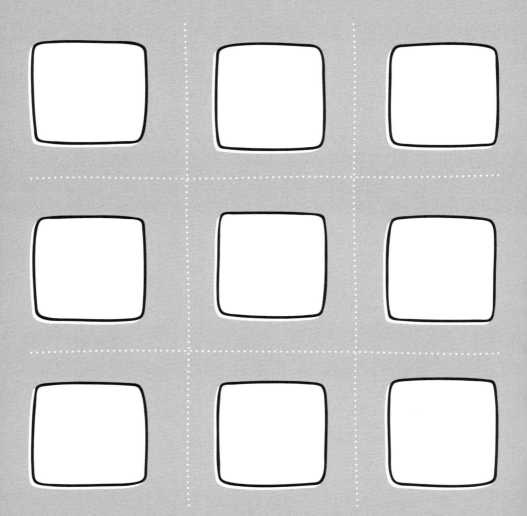

WRITE your favorite passage in the Bible and why it is meaningful to you. (150)

_____
_____
_____
_____
_____
_____
_____
_____
_____
_____
_____
_____
_____
_____
_____
_____
_____
_____
_____
_____
_____

151 **QUICK DRAW!** Sketch the first thing that pops into your head in less than a minute. Use a timer.

ARTIST TIP:
When coloring, don't press too hard. Your tools will last longer.

DRAW the sun and the moon seven different ways.

"For you, a thousand years are as a passing day, as brief as a few night hours."

PSALM 90:4 NLT

FILL the page with art supplies, no two alike.

"Now he who supplies seed to the sower and bread for food will also supply and increase your store of seed and will enlarge the harvest of your righteousness."

2 CORINTHIANS 9:10 NIV

MAKE a picture by coloring the squares.

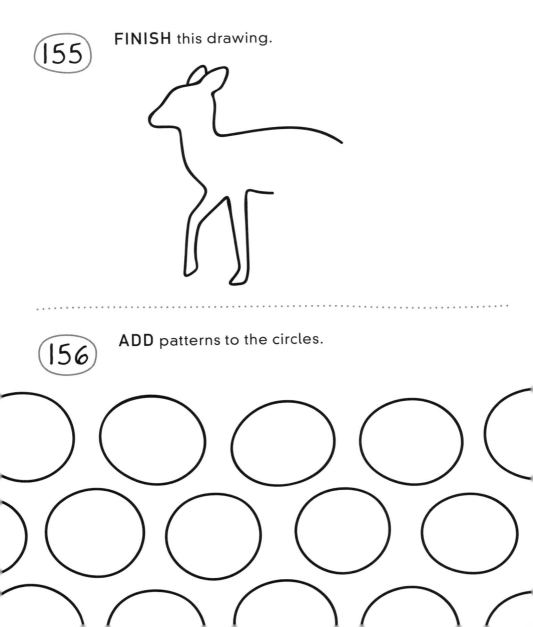

155 FINISH this drawing.

156 ADD patterns to the circles.

DRAW a scene from your favorite book or movie.

· ·

DRAW a light source, such as a flashlight or lamp.

"When Jesus spoke again to the people, he said, 'I am the light of the world. Whoever follows me will never walk in darkness, but will have the light of life.'"

JOHN 8:12 NIV

(159) **WRITE** about your favorite three of God's creations.

① _____
_____
_____

② _____
_____
_____

③ _____
_____
_____

"Everything God created is good, and nothing is to be rejected
if it is received with thanksgiving."

1 TIMOTHY 4:4 NIV

PICK a photograph you are fond of. DRAW what you see. WRITE a caption explaining why this brings you joy.

COLOR this word. **ADD** some doodles of your own.

DRAW a picture using only rectangles.

CONNECT the dots however you like to form an image.

"God has made everything beautiful for its own time. He has planted eternity in the human heart, but even so, people cannot see the whole scope of God's work from beginning to end."

ECCLESIASTES 3:11 NLT

COLOR the picture.

165

DRAW a lamp and **ADD** spots, stripes, eyeballs, fur, wings, or whatever your imagination comes up with!

167 COLOR around the Scripture.

"The name of the LORD is a fortified tower;
the righteous run to it and are safe."

PROVERBS 18:10 NIV

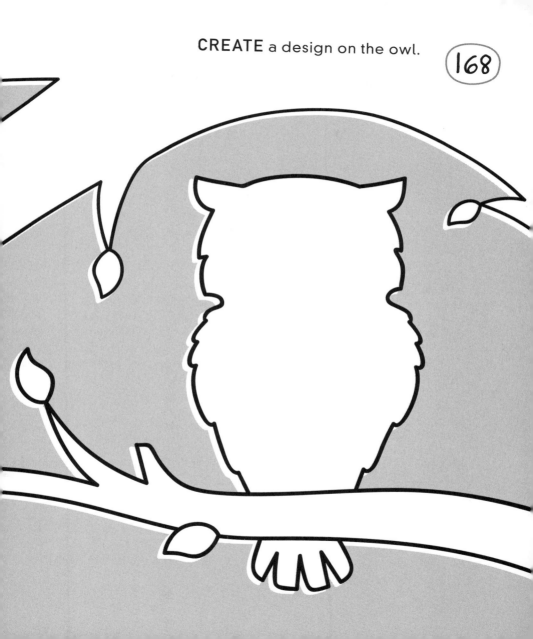

FREE DRAW! Draw whatever you want today.

People-watching time! **SIT** somewhere in public and **FIND** someone doing something positive. **WRITE** about it.

_____

_____

_____

_____

_____

_____

_____

_____

_____

_____

_____

_____

_____

_____

_____

"Be shepherds of God's flock that is under your care, watching over them—not because you must, but because you are willing."

1 PETER 5:2 NIV

DRAW a peaceful landscape.

171

"Consider the blameless, observe the upright;
a future awaits those who seek peace."

PSALM 37:37 NIV

Imagine your shoes can talk. **WRITE** what they would say.

FILL the page with birds, no two alike.

COLOR the footprints in a way that reminds you of a beautiful place you've seen.

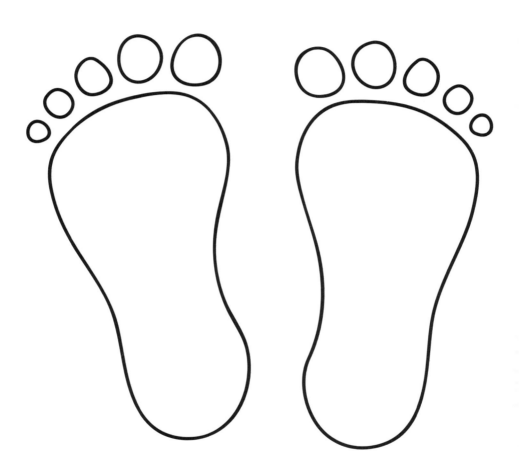

"Since we live by the Spirit, let us keep in step with the Spirit."

GALATIANS 5:25 NIV

Pretend God had made you something other than human. **DRAW** what that could be.

179

DRAW different weather patterns on the clouds.

DRAW your favorite season.

"There is a time for everything, and a season for every
activity under the heavens."

ECCLESIASTES 3:1 NIV

CONNECT the dots however you like to form an image.

"We don't look at the troubles we can see now; rather, we fix our gaze on things that cannot be seen. For the things we see now will soon be gone, but the things we cannot see will last forever."

2 CORINTHIANS 4:18 NLT

185 **WRITE** a prayer for a cause that is meaningful to you.

_____

_____

_____

_____

_____

_____

_____

_____

_____

_____

_____

_____

_____

_____

_____

_____

_____

DRAW something you are proud of.

DRAW an animal family.

"Start children off on the way they should go,
and even when they are old they will not turn from it."

PROVERBS 22:6 NIV

"Be strong. Be strong in heart,
all you who hope in the Lord."

PSALM 31:24 NLV

CREATE a design on the deer.

WRITE about something you wish to improve on.

_____

_____

_____

_____

_____

_____

_____

_____

_____

_____

_____

_____

_____

_____

"Whoever heeds discipline shows the way to life,
but whoever ignores correction leads others astray."

PROVERBS 10:17 NIV

PRACTICE drawing feet in several different positions.

ARTIST TIP:
Let in some natural light. It's good for the mind and spirit.

MAKE a picture by coloring the triangles.

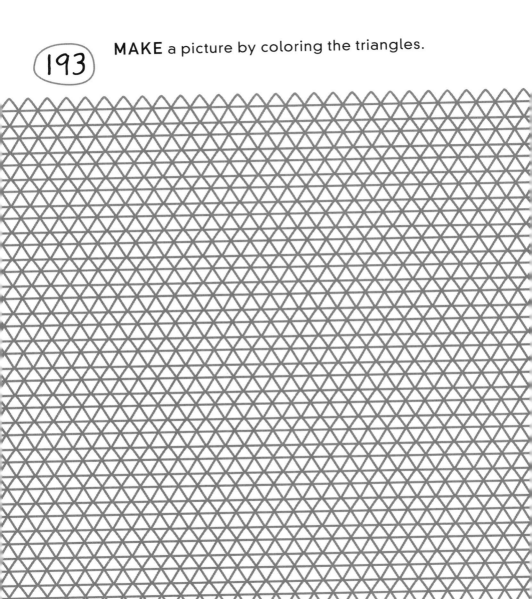

FILL the page with hats, no two alike.

DRAW a phone large and **ADD** spots, stripes, eyeballs, fur, wings, or whatever your imagination comes up with!

WRITE a new ending to a book or movie you love.

_____

_____

_____

_____

_____

_____

_____

_____

_____

_____

_____

_____

_____

_____

_____

_____

_____

_____

_____

DRAW labels for your favorite foods on the jars.

DRAW a path to somewhere beautiful. (198)

"Show me your ways, LORD, teach me your paths."

FREE DRAW! Create whatever you want today.

COLOR the picture. 200

COLOR this word.

"As water reflects the face,
so one's life reflects the heart."

PROVERBS 27:19 NIV

CONNECT the dots however you like to form an image.

ADD a body to the fox. 204

WRITE three things you would do with one billion dollars.

1 _____

_____

_____

2 _____

_____

_____

3 _____

_____

_____

"How beautiful on the mountains are the feet of him who brings good news, who tells of peace and brings good news of happiness, who tells of saving power, and says to Zion, 'Your God rules!'"

ISAIAH 52:7 NLV

207 DRAW something that makes you happy.

DRAW patterns on the fruit.

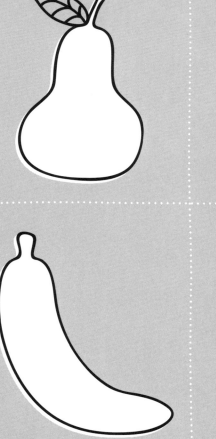

Most complicated art contains some basic shapes.
CREATE an animal or person using this rectangle.

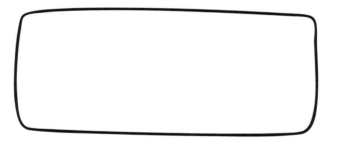

COLOR around the Scripture.

211

"Praise be to the God and Father of our Lord Jesus Christ, the Father of compassion and the God of all comfort, who comforts us in all our troubles, so that we can comfort those in any trouble with the comfort we ourselves receive from God."

2 CORINTHIANS 1:3-4 NIV

DRAW and COLOR something abstract that makes you feel hopeful.

ARTIST TIP:
Break the rules. Coloring outside the lines and getting messy can help you grow.

MAKE a picture by coloring the stars.

DRAW a self-portrait...with your eyes closed.

"We live by faith, not by sight."

2 CORINTHIANS 5:7 NIV

217 Anything can be given character. **DRAW** a pair of glasses large and **ADD** spots, stripes, eyeballs, fur, wings, or whatever your imagination comes up with!

ARTIST TIP:
Experiment with different textures to add richness to your page.

CREATE something using only circles.

219

Set a timer. **LIST** as many of your blessings as you can in one minute.

1 _____

2 _____

3 _____

4 _____

5 _____

6 _____

7 _____

8 _____

9 _____

10 _____

11 _____

12 _____

13 _____

14 _____

15 _____

16 _____

17 _____

18 _____

19 _____

20 _____

21 _____

22 _____

23 _____

24 _____

25 _____

26 _____

27 _____

28 _____

WRITE as many gracious words as you can think of in the honeycomb. 220

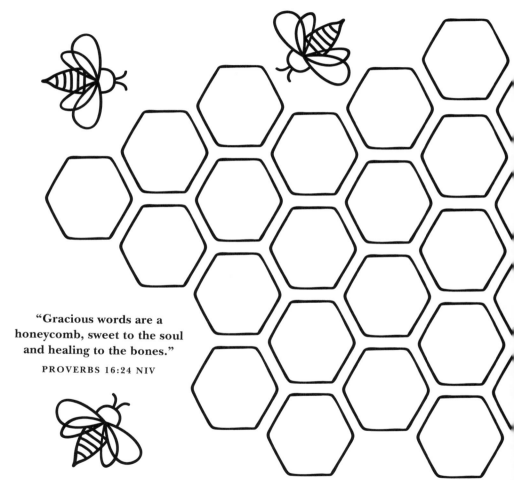

"Gracious words are a honeycomb, sweet to the soul and healing to the bones."

PROVERBS 16:24 NIV

COLOR this word.

CONNECT the dots however you like to form an image.

"Yours, O Lord, is the greatness, the power and the glory, the victory
and the majesty; for all that is in heaven and in earth is Yours;
Yours is the kingdom, O Lord, and You are exalted as head over all."

1 CHRONICLES 29:11 NKJV

225 **WRITE** about a time you've been proud of yourself.

_____

_____

_____

_____

_____

_____

_____

_____

_____

_____

_____

_____

_____

_____

FILL the page with trees, no two alike.

MAKE a picture by coloring the hexagons.

CREATE a design on the swan.

229 **DRAW** something worth more than material things.

"I tell you, do not worry about your life, what you will eat or drink; or about your body, what you will wear. Is not life more than food, and the body more than clothes?"

MATTHEW 6:25 NIV

PRACTICE drawing mouths with different expressions.

COLOR the picture.

232

FILL this page with socks, no two alike.

"Do not fear, for I am with you.
Do not be afraid, for I am your God.
I will give you strength, and for sure I
will help you. Yes, I will hold you up with
My right hand that is right and good."

ISAIAH 41:10 NLV

MAKE a picture by coloring the shapes.

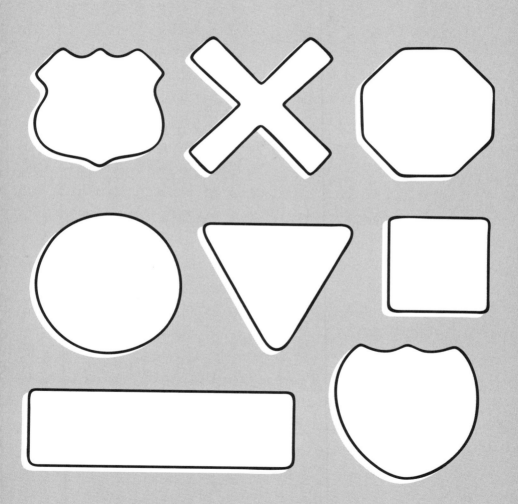

237 Imagine you were given one miracle.
WRITE what you would ask for.

_____

_____

_____

_____

_____

_____

_____

_____

_____

_____

_____

_____

_____

_____

_____

DRAW your ideal garden.

ARTIST TIP:
Art supply stores have thousands of fun materials,
but masterpieces have been created with just a pencil.

239 **FREE DRAW!** Draw whatever you want today.

CREATE designs on the watering cans.

DRAW a peaceful pillow to sleep in with.

"A loud and cheerful greeting early in the morning will be taken as a curse!"

PROVERBS 27:14 NLT

CONNECT the dots however you like to form an image.

ADD one of your favorite people to this hammock. (244)

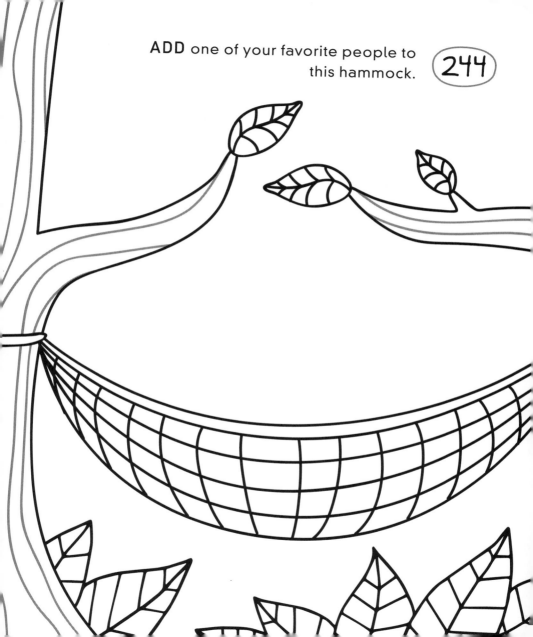

245 CREATE something using this Scripture as inspiration.

"The LORD is good to all, and His tender mercies are over all His works."

PSALM 145:9 NKJV

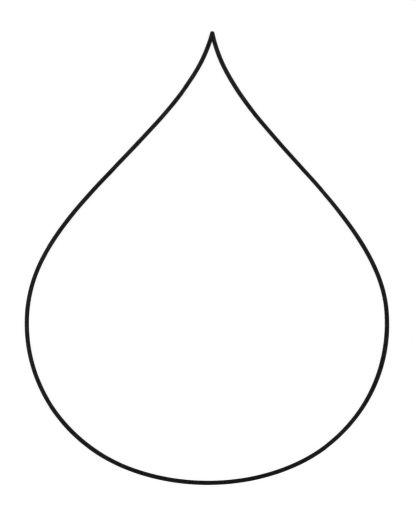

DRAW and color something abstract that makes you feel excited.

ADD a woodgrain texture and color to the birdhouse.

248

249 **WRITE** about a time your generosity has come back to you in a positive way.

_____
_____
_____
_____
_____
_____
_____
_____
_____
_____
_____
_____
_____
_____
_____

"A generous person will prosper; whoever refreshes others will be refreshed."

PROVERBS 11:25 NIV

COLOR the picture.

250

251 COLOR this picture without using the color yellow.

FILL the page with butterflies, no two alike.

253 **CREATE** something using only squares.

"Peace I leave with you; my peace
I give you. I do not give to you as the
world gives. Do not let your hearts be
troubled and do not be afraid."

JOHN 14:27 NIV

255 Most complicated art contains some basic shapes. **CREATE** an animal or person using this oval.

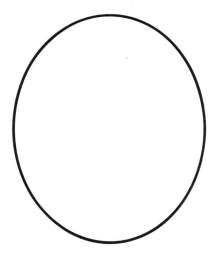

MAKE a picture by coloring the octagons.

FINISH this drawing.

_____
_____
_____
_____
_____
_____
_____
_____
_____
_____
_____
_____
_____
_____
_____
_____
_____

COLOR this word.

DRAW a basket of bread.

(260)

"Then Jesus declared, 'I am the bread of life. Whoever comes to me will never go hungry, and whoever believes in me will never be thirsty.'"

JOHN 6:35 NIV

261

If you could turn water into anything, **WRITE** what it would be. What would you do with this power?

_____

_____

_____

_____

_____

_____

_____

_____

_____

_____

_____

_____

_____

_____

_____

_____

_____

_____

DRAW lily pads on a pond.

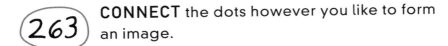

263 CONNECT the dots however you like to form an image.

DESIGN a series of stamps.

CREATE something using this Scripture as inspiration.

"When you eat the labor of your hands, you shall be happy, and it shall be well with you."

PSALM 128:2 NKJV

COLOR the picture.

266

GO NUTS! Scribble wildly all over this page.

ARTIST TIP:
If you're frustrated with a certain medium, such as paint or pottery, try another. There are many ways to make art.

FREE DRAW! Draw whatever you want today.

DRAW a park scene around this bench. 270

MAKE a picture by coloring the shapes.

FILL the page with cups, no two alike.

272

273 **DRAW** an apple and **ADD** spots, stripes, eyeballs, fur, wings, or whatever your imagination comes up with!

....

274 **CREATE** a postcard of your favorite place.

COLOR around the Scripture.

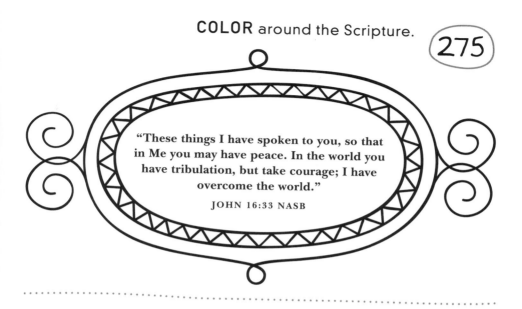

"These things I have spoken to you, so that in Me you may have peace. In the world you have tribulation, but take courage; I have overcome the world."

JOHN 16:33 NASB

DRAW your favorite treats from a bakery. 276

WRITE your favorite quote in the clouds.

_____

_____

_____

_____

_____

_____

_____

_____

_____

_____

_____

_____

_____

_____

_____

_____

"LORD, be merciful to me; heal my soul, for I have sinned against You."

PSALM 41:4 NKJV

ADD something from nature.

279

DRAW a place where you'd like to retire.

DRAW fireworks in the sky.

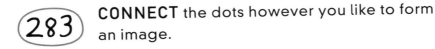

CONNECT the dots however you like to form an image.

"Happy are the people whose God is the Lord!"

PSALM 144:15 NKJV

285

WRITE about your hopes and prayers for someone you love.

_____

_____

_____

_____

_____

_____

_____

_____

_____

_____

_____

_____

_____

_____

_____

_____

DRAW yourself in clothing from another era.

DRAW or write about something you do on Sundays.

"God blessed the seventh day and made it holy, because on it he rested from all the work of creating that he had done."

GENESIS 2:3 NIV

MAKE a picture by coloring the octagons.

FILL the page with bees, no two alike.

291 **FINISH** this drawing. **ADD** something fun to the basket.

DRAW and **COLOR** something abstract that helps you to feel calm.

COLOR this word.

PRACTICE drawing hair in different styles.

295 **CREATE** something using only triangles.

CHOOSE a photograph from your albums and write the story behind it.

_____
_____
_____
_____
_____
_____
_____
_____
_____
_____
_____
_____
_____
_____
_____
_____
_____
_____
_____

297

COLOR around the Scripture.

"God is our refuge and strength, an ever-present help in trouble."

PSALM 46:1 NIV

DRAW your favorite holiday.

FREE DRAW! Draw whatever you want today.

COLOR this picture without using the color blue.

DRAW a boat on the water.

ARTIST TIP:
Try mixing materials. There's no rule for using
only one or a dozen different materials in art.

CONNECT the dots however you like to form an image.

"Bless those who curse you, pray for those who mistreat you."

LUKE 6:28 NIV

305

How are you? **ANSWER** this question with a paragraph.

_____

_____

_____

_____

_____

_____

_____

_____

_____

_____

_____

_____

_____

_____

_____

DRAW something very large next to something very small.

309 FILL the page with ants, no two alike.

ARTIST TIP:
Drawing is a skill developed over time.
No one is born knowing how to draw.

DRAW a cupcake large and **ADD** spots, stripes, eyeballs, fur, wings, or whatever your imagination comes up with!

MAKE a picture by coloring the rectangles.

Complicated art usually contains some basic elements. **CREATE** an animal or person using these lines.

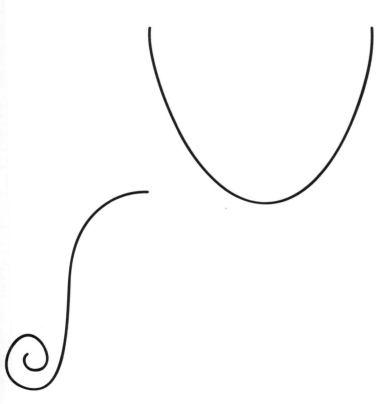

DRAW something you find in a farmers market.

COLOR the picture.

315

DRAW a scene from a funny animal video you saw online.

DRAW an outfit you would gift to a friend.

"The Spirit God gave us does not make us timid, but gives us power, love and self-discipline."

2 TIMOTHY 1:7 NIV

WRITE about someone or something that inspires you.

_____

_____

_____

_____

_____

_____

_____

_____

_____

_____

_____

_____

_____

_____

_____

DRAW something you have loved from childhood.

COLOR this word.

DRAW yourself doing something fun with your best friend. (322)

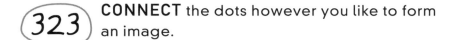

323 **CONNECT** the dots however you like to form an image.

"Isaac planted crops in that land and the same year reaped a hundredfold, because the LORD blessed him."

GENESIS 26:12 NIV

DRAW places you have been in the frames.

FILL the page with colorful rocks, no two alike. (326)

327

DRAW a cheerful heart.

"A cheerful heart is good medicine, but a broken spirit saps a person's strength."

PROVERBS 17:22 NLT

DESIGN a matching set of garden tools.

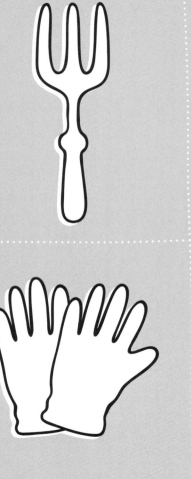

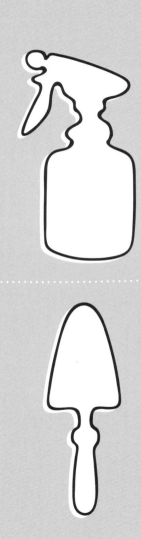

DRAW someone in God's hands.

"God will wipe away every tear from their eyes; there shall be no more death, nor sorrow, nor crying. There shall be no more pain, for the former things have passed away."

REVELATION 21:4 NKJV

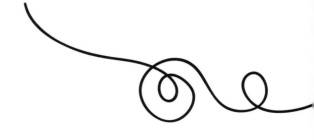

COLOR the picture.

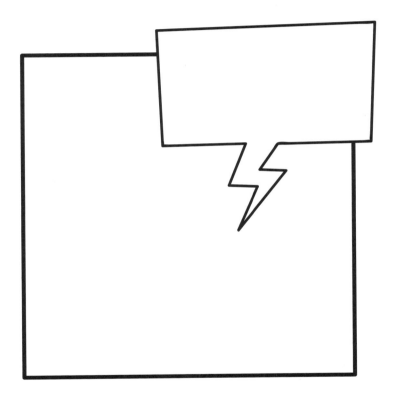

CREATE a new recipe and write it down here.

_____
_____
_____
_____
_____
_____
_____
_____
_____
_____
_____
_____
_____
_____
_____
_____
_____
_____
_____

COLOR around the Scripture.

"Cast your burden upon the LORD
and He will sustain you;
He will never allow the righteous
to be shaken."

PSALM 55:22 NASB

WRITE three things that help you relax and bring you to your happy place. (338)

1 _____
_____
_____

2 _____
_____
_____

3 _____
_____
_____

MAKE a picture by coloring the shapes.

FILL this page with faces, no two alike.

FREE DRAW! Create whatever you want today.

COLOR the picture.

342

343 **CONNECT** the dots however you like to form an image.

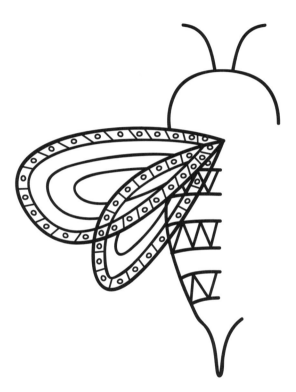

"Then God said, 'Let us make mankind in our image, in our likeness, so that they may rule over the fish in the sea and the birds in the sky, over the livestock and all the wild animals, and over all the creatures that move along the ground.'"

GENESIS 1:26 NIV

CREATE something using this Scripture as inspiration.

"Be kind and compassionate to one another, forgiving each other, just as in Christ God forgave you."

EPHESIANS 4:32 NIV

347 DRAW yourself as you were in the past, as you are in the present, and how you hope to be in the future.

349

WRITE a prayer for a friend.

_____

_____

_____

_____

_____

_____

_____

_____

_____

_____

_____

_____

_____

_____

_____

"Dear friend, I hope all is well with you and that you are as healthy in body as you are strong in spirit."

3 JOHN 2 NLT

351 **DRAW** a basket full of your favorite things.

COLOR this picture without using the color red or green. (352)

MAKE a picture by coloring the hearts.

If you could create a new species, **DRAW** what it would look like.

DRAW a celebration.

 **COLOR** this picture without using the color orange.

COLOR around the Scripture. 357

"I call on the LORD
in my distress, and he
answers me."

PSALM 120:1 NIV

DRAW someone dancing. 358

359

WRITE three good things that happened this year.

1 _____
_____
_____

2 _____
_____
_____

3 _____
_____
_____

361 **CREATE** something using this Scripture as inspiration.

"LORD, our LORD, how majestic is your name in all the earth!
You have set your glory in the heavens."

PSALM 8:1 NIV

CREATE a design on the bear.

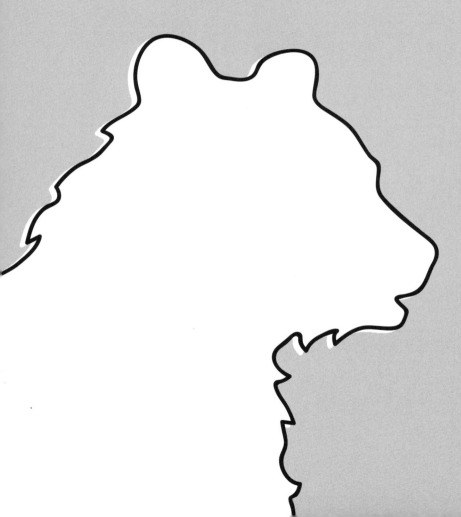

FILL this page with frogs, no two alike.

365 **USE** this as a page to test colors or materials.

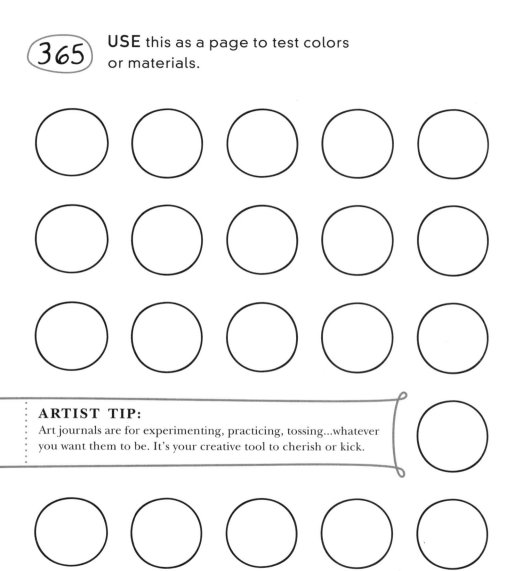

ARTIST TIP:
Art journals are for experimenting, practicing, tossing...whatever you want them to be. It's your creative tool to cherish or kick.